I0830285

Bridging the Gap

How to Reach Today's Workforce

David G. Matthews

authorHOUSE

AuthorHouse™
1663 Liberty Drive
Bloomington, IN 47403
www.authorhouse.com
Phone: 1 (800) 839-8640

© 2020 David G. Matthews. All rights reserved.

No part of this book may be reproduced, stored in a retrieval system, or transmitted by any means without the written permission of the author.

Published by AuthorHouse 12/26/2019

ISBN: 978-1-7283-4090-6 (sc)
ISBN: 978-1-7283-4091-3 (e)

Print information available on the last page.

Any people depicted in stock imagery provided by Getty Images are models, and such images are being used for illustrative purposes only.
Certain stock imagery © Getty Images.

This book is printed on acid-free paper.

Because of the dynamic nature of the Internet, any web addresses or links contained in this book may have changed since publication and may no longer be valid. The views expressed in this work are solely those of the author and do not necessarily reflect the views of the publisher, and the publisher hereby disclaims any responsibility for them.

CONTENTS

Preface vii
Introduction ix

Chapter 1   The Backstory 1
            Humility 4
            My Turn 5

Chapter 2   The role of a Front-line Manager 9
            What is a Manager 9
            What is the focus of a Manager 11
            Why are Managers Needed 16

Chapter 3   Challenges and Successes of Managers 17
            Daily Operations 17
            How to Manage my Manager 19
            How to Win 20

Chapter 4   What makes a "good" Manager 23
            Know your People 23
            Have a clear and well defined plan 25
            Know your business and have compassion 27

Chapter 5   The Role of a Teacher................................ 29
             Setting the Tone...................................... 29
             Planning 30
             Creating a healthy environment 31

Chapter 6   What makes a "good" Teacher 33
             Compassion.. 33
             Trust & Integrity 34
             Inspiration 35

Chapter 7   The Concept!....................................... 37
             What is it! 37
             Why 39

Appendix 43
Appendix 2 49
Failure Mode Effect Analysis.................................51
References.. 55
About the Author... 57

The purpose of this book is to open the minds of traditional thinkers about how certain skill sets do or don't translate to other work streams. During the past six years, I have interviewed countless people that have had great skills but did not translate to the work stream they were applying for. As the interviewer was questioned, it became apparent to me that we were targeting the wrong kind of candidate. In Supply Chain, you look for Supply Chain minded individuals. This methodology has worked and does work but often times the better candidate does not apply because of traditional thinking. When Supply Chain professionals are asked to "look" outside of Supply Chain to find someone with fresh ideas only a few industries are ever looked into. Manufacturing is an industry that is looked at for getting managers and leaders that have a different outlook on operations and that have a drive for the details.

Thinking about the logic of why the Manufacturing industry is pulled upon makes sense. The leaders are accustomed to having to complete work orders, making some part or product to specification with minimal variation, reporting hourly and speaking to gaps in performance. This is very similar to what is needed in Supply Chain. In this book, you will read about my concept of using Teachers as Supply Chain professionals. Teachers are detailed. Teachers have to be specific with lesson planning and they have accountability tailored to them and the school if they miss on educational focal points. They understand the importance that every child is unique and while the lesson plan may not tailored to that child specifically, their are programs and support that can be given to that child to help them meet educational goals. Imagine if this type of thinking, drive for excellence, ownership of their classroom, and care for their children was represented in a Supply Chain Supervisor or Area Manager. What would your turnover look like? What would your Engagement Scores reflect? Think about manager calibration and how much more challenging that would be when this type of leader enters the manager pool. This book will unpack this concept and the benefits of having this type of leader. We hope you enjoy.

INTRODUCTION

Being a leader is a daunting task. Several people look to you for direction, for approval, for praise, and often it's a relationship where the leader gives more than they receive. Some managers are often frustrated with an ever changing environment and limited tools to help them adapt and adjust to the needs of the business and the associates in which they manage. I have lived this personally and seen this firsthand as I have managed front-line managers through the grey areas of operation. The associates also feel their own frustrations as they adapt to the environment and to the leader. Through conversations with associates I have learned that they do want to perform well but their leader doesn't listen to them. Or their leader doesn't hold people accountable fairly. Sometimes I hear that their leader doesn't know what to do and the decisions they are making causes us to not finish and carry over workloads. The sad truth is all of the frustrations listed and not listed by the manager and the associates are true.

Whether you are doing well, or your career is collapsing right around you, most people desire to become better managers. The question is How? How do I become a better manager? What can I do to become a better manager? What must I do to gain a better understanding of the operation and Supply Chain so that I can lead my team safely and efficiently with the right focus in mind. I want to help you do just that. In this book, I hope you gain insight on some of the successes and challenges managers have which should show you that you are not alone. The "you" in this case is both the manager and the employer. I will also introduce a concept that should help every front-line manager and supervisor take their current skill set to another level using tools we all have seen and experienced.

Get ready! This journey you are about to embark is eye opening and life changing for some. Although promises cannot be made, I am certain that if the practices of the concept I propose are used as described, your career as a manager will flourish as you gain a deeper understanding of the business, processes, develop meaningful and lasting relationships, and spark a flame in you and in others that cannot be put out.

CHAPTER 1

The Backstory

What quality do great star players have? What makes them stand out? Is it their exceptional coordination of hand and eye? Is it their ability to inspire the team and create a force of movement so great the game winning shot is made? We have seen athletes like Brady, Aikman and Bradshaw win games like this time and time again. So, what is it? How are they able to be so successful? Maybe it's the countless hours of physical training coupled with video study and scrutiny from their coaches on every play. Is it their ability to rally the team and keep them focused on the offensive play? Is it the team believing in their ability and their teammate's ability to execute? Maybe, it's all those things. As I think about what qualities make a great player, I relate this thought to what makes a good leader. Many of us do the same. Millions of dollars and thousands of books have been written contrasting professional athletes and their ability to plan, communicate, execute, and lead a team to the workforce. Clearly there is a gap in the workforce that people are searching to find a way to close. In this book, you will read and understand the industry viewpoint on what a good leader is and my concept to bridge the gap from where leaders currently are to better leaders.

When I was 19, I worked for a company to support myself through college. I was a pretty good athlete in high school, so hard work didn't bother me. In fact, I welcomed hard work. I knew that hard work, persistence, and creative thinking would help me grow with his company. While working, I thought the work I was doing was ok, it wasn't hard and in fact kind of easy. I would hear other workers complain about the working conditions, the environment, management and so on, but I didn't let that phase me. I guess I was too young professionally to understand why my peers had gripes with the leadership. I was so new I didn't join the conversation, but I listened. Key point, in your operations today, there are people that are talking about perceived problems and there are people listening. As leaders, it is important to have a good understanding of the pulse of the people so that the right information is communicated to the workforce and employee concerns can be addressed.

As I watched and listened, I felt the people I was working with didn't get the big picture and I felt they were entitled. I was so used to hearing my coaches talk about the team and the greater good of the team, I didn't realize some of the emotions and feelings these workers had because of how decisions impacted them and their families. These people have families to take care of and bills of a greater magnitude of mine at that time, so I assumed the employees were yapping at the mouth and didn't understand what the supervisor was wanting them to do.

The longer I worked for this company, the more I learned about bad supervision and how employees are treated and mentally broken down because of clique or social status. This was becoming too political for me and I didn't want any part of it. Just let us work, pay us fairly, talk to us with some sense, and when you see your employees struggling help us, don't continue to sit in the office. This situation lite a fire in me and I thought I could promote to a supervisor make some changes. I assumed that since I learned the operation and I know it better than my supervisor, I could lead the team. Has anyone else felt that way. As I worked in the operation I knew exactly what was wrong and how to fix it. What I didn't realize was how narrow of a focus I had at that time. I felt like if "they" would just listen to me and follow my lead we will increase productivity, pay the workers more, and solve all of the company's problems. If anyone feels this way or has associates that think in this manner here is my suggestion. Have a roundtable meeting with them and discuss the issues. Most things and fixable or at least understandable. The key is to have open lines of communication. This didn't happen for me in this situation. I had a lot to learn about myself, about leaders, and about how this company solves problems. My approach to solve this problem was to promote to a supervisor and be in a position to make changes. That may seem off base to some but for me it was directly on point. I took the approach if you want change, become change. The only thing was, I didn't have the slightest idea about how to lead people. Being a captain on a football and baseball team is different. The stakes are higher now and my decision impact people's lives. I had to quickly learn how to lead and how to do it effectively. I had tenacity and I had a knack for figuring out problems and making things work, but I was missing so much more. I applied for the position and I was awarded the supervisors role. From then to now, I have changed as a leader 100-fold and hopefully as you read this book, your thinking will change too.

Humility

My first few weeks in the company were the least bit stellar for me. I was supposed to train on a machine as an operator, but they had other plans for me. I was asked to sweep the warehouse from front to back and that was my only job. I felt, "they" were trying to break me. Have you heard employees say that or voice they feel that way? At least, that's what it seemed like to me. I would see the supervisor maybe once per day as I swept. I didn't get any follow up on next steps for me to get training on the machine for which I was hired to do. I was just sweeping. I swept the entire building, a five hundred fifty thousand square feet manufacturing warehouse with areas that were not swept in years. As I began my task of sweeping, I made an agreement with myself to not quit and look at this task as a challenge. I was not going to let this get the best of me. When I started and realized I didn't have adequate tools to clean the area, this task could quickly overwhelm me, and I would be sweeping for weeks. So, I made it a point to get done as quickly as I could be using every resource and tool I could. I wanted to get trained on the machine because that's where the higher paying jobs where. As I swept the building with inventory in places that hadn't moved in years, I saw this challenge as one that would be a defining moment. Either I was going to learn a lesson or quit, and quitting wasn't an option.

It took me two weeks, 8 hours a day for four days straight to sweep this place (it looked better honestly) then I went to the machine. I knew if I could get on the machine, life would be better. I asked the supervisor to let me get to the machine for training but I noticed hesitation. He even started to give me other jobs to do that were not on the machine. After my weeks of sweeping, cleaning, taking lunch outside of the normal lunch period because I was on "special projects." I had enough of that. I told myself that I would leaned everything this operator could teach me, so I would never go back to a job like that. I asked the supervisor if I was approved to work overtime, so I could work with the other operators on other shifts and gain more knowledge. He thought my request was for more hours and untimely a bigger check. I explained to him my goal was to learn quickly so I could become more valuable. I learned at an early age to grow from the mistakes of others, so more time with more operators meant more knowledge; and knowledge is power.

My Turn

Fast-forward one year, I was promoted from operator, to lead operator, and then Front-Line Supervisor. I was 20 years old and I finally arrived! So, I thought. I traded in my coveralls for some slacks and a button-down shirt, fresh haircut and a clipboard. From my narrow view as an operator looking at past supervisors I assumed this would be a piece of cake. I mean, the hard part is working on the machines not managing and leading the people. That part is easy right?

How many of your associates say that to you? As many of us know, this is far from the truth. Leading people can be challenging and rewarding at the same time. Through my years of management, I learned situational management techniques that have helped me alter my style of management to the situation. During this time of my professional career I was learning humility, learning how to make a connection with the workforce, and how to deliver results.

Since I worked with these associates as a peer to them, I had a good sense of what the team ultimately needed, and I understood what some of the associates were going through and could also articulate what management needed. There was a clear lack of trust from the associate level to management and the sooner I could fix that, my days became easier. I knew the associates were not performing where they could and where they should. Not knowing exactly how to solve this problem I knew the associates had the answer, so I had my very first stand down. I pulled each associate off the floor one by one and had a candid conversation with them. As a rule, always have HR present in these types of conversations. HR is a business partner and will help you rather than hurt you. They have a vested interest in seeing the success of the associate and management staff.

As I had these conversations, I started off by telling the people that once trained me on the machines that their jobs where not in jeopardy. Surprisingly to me, many of the people I spoke with felt that now that I was a Supervisor I had some hidden agenda to get rid of them. That wasn't true. Once clearing the air, the conversations went smoothly, and we were able to talk openly. Lesson learned here was to be open and honest with the associates. They will respect you more if you don't treat them like they don't matter or don't understand, be real with them. At the end of the one on one's, I was able to get the entire workforce aligned and moving in the right direction. I was upfront with them and they were upfront with me. I told them what the expectations were for them and I even asked them what support they need for me. Asking the associates what support they need from me was unheard at that time. "You mean, you want me to tell you what support you can give me"? Anyone watching this would have thought Christmas came and I was passing out gifts. One operator told me to give him the opportunity to fail. This was scary for me at first, but it did make sense. I need to trust my people and they must trust me. That was the point of the meeting, right? Fix the trust between associates and supervisor. So, this began my learning of how to lead people. As a manager, you will have people that genuinely want to succeed, but they may not know how. As a leader, you should know that your success comes by having them succeed so you have a vested interest in helping your associates win…. get the point!

Over the next several years I grew as a leader and it wasn't easy. Some people have learned their style leadership and how their skills fits in with the organization, but many managers feel like they don't fit. In speaking with several managers, I get the sense they are in a role where they are not using their strongest attribute and that is uncomfortable for them. Here is the problem, there is no one size fits all solution. When managers leave departments for various reasons, companies have periods of struggle due to the change in management… Stick close to the upcoming sections and you will understand from a company perspective how to position yourself to prevent the swings in operation because of manager shift.

CHAPTER 2

The role of a Front-line Manager

What is a Manager

When leaders take on a new role, often they have a skill that helped them stand out or some knowledge of the next role and they can do some of that job. For me, I was skilled at execution. I was very task driven and I was blessed with the ability to use creative thinking to get things done. I didn't know exactly what a supervisor was, but I felt I could get things done. I knew how to leverage people and systems as needed to fix issues that I saw from an associate perspective. What I saw was done by my supervisor when I was an hourly associate was limited and biased. I assumed all he did was sit in his office and occasionally come to the production area and ask questions validating he doesn't have a clue as to what we are doing.

I soon came to learn, there is much more involved when you have the responsibility of leading people within an organization. I can say my training was more of a job shadow for a week then off I go as a full fledge supervisor. Really?! A week of training was all I am going to get? How do I manage time and attendance? What to do when the person tells me they want to use cash in PTO (Personal Time Off) time and they are wanting to work OT (Over Time) because they have bills due, but we are cutting hours? How do I handle that? What do I say? I had some bumps and bruises during the beginning stages of my career in management. During those days Google was less than a year old and Wikipedia didn't exist, so I couldn't ask the masses and learn what I needed to do. I had to humble myself and ask my manager and other managers what being a manager was all about. Learning to navigate through what a Manager is was no easy task. Being a Manager is a lifestyle. It is more than coming to work and checking the box. It is caring for you people and the organization and doing everything you can to find balance and deliver results for both entities.

How many people can answer this question right now without looking it up? What is the role of a Front-line manager? I am certain that if fifteen people are paneled, we will get fifteen different answers. Sure, there will be some similar but again, this isn't one size fits all and it shouldn't be, however, there should be some common ground. What is the common ground for front-line leaders? For starters, it's how you treat people. Millions of dollars are spent yearly training leaders on soft skills because it's just that important. Before anything happens in operations, the associates have already sized up the manager or supervisor and have decided if they want to work for them or not largely based on how the associates are treated. Believe it or don't believe it, its true. People want to work for a supervisor that cares about them or at least will fight for them when they can't fight for themselves. What kind of supervisor are you, or what kind of supervisors do you employ? Are you or your leaders defending your associates when it matters, or are associates calling out from work and leaving early for reasons unknown to the leadership. Supervisors and Managers are more than messengers and it's time to truly understand what that means. They are the champions of the organization and through them, bottom-lines are achieved, moral is improved, development is attained, and something special happens. We win!

What is the focus of a Manager

Across many sectors of business and types of work, the role of a manager can differ in many ways. In today's environment, a front line manager is defined as, "First or second level managers (line managers, office managers, supervisors) directly responsible for <u>production</u> of <u>goods and services</u>, and supervision of clerical <u>staff</u> and <u>shop floor</u> employees. "(2). Some managers are more tactical and direct than others and that could be because of the environment or the needs of the team at that time. While other managers can plan, coach, and manipulate the operation through its employees as a result of the culture of the company and the skill set of the leader. No matter what type of manager you are, every manager faces challenges that can make or break them.

I had to learn what my role was in a few short weeks at a very early age in my career. I figured out that if I provided structure to team, help them understand where defects are being made and what actions should be taken to correct, apply pressure (accountability) where needed, and do not mess up payroll, I would be successful. No better way to destroy your credibly with the associates is be a manager without a plan, don't understand the process well enough to help the operation, show favoritism and not drive accountability, and cause mutiny by not paying associates accurately, timely, and fairly. This is a recipe for disaster.

As an associate, I remember my supervisor coming to me or my peers with a plan and quickly get shut down because he forgot a key factor in the operation. The supervisor lost credibility with the associates because of a lack of knowledge about the process within the operation. It became very difficult for the supervisor to ask for tasks to be completed because the associates would say, "this doesn't make sense" and do it anyway knowing it would fail. Does this sound familiar? I have also see the supervisor lose credibility with the associates when they don't handle behavioral situations promptly and correctly. Here is an example of what I mean. An associate named Sarah goes to the manager asking them why another associate is always in an indirect role such as a clerk. In that moment the supervisor can make or break the trust of this associate. Take a moment and discuss how you or your team would handle this situation. In this case, the supervisor told the associate that it was his decision to place people in support roles and if they had an issue with this, they can see the department manager. Wrong, wrong, wrong! When this finally escalated to my attention, I had to explain to the associate our policy for job assignments and job rotation. This understanding cleared up the concern for the associate, but it was evident job rotation wasn't happening. That was something tangible that could be fixed. The supervisor and department manager were both coached on how to handle situations like this. It takes just a few moments to explain so that understanding can be realized vs. blowing someone off creating a host of other issues.

During my career, I have learned at a more in-depth level of what a front-line manager's role is. I have debated certain aspects of their role whether its achievable but an expectation nonetheless. As I have managed font-line managers and have been one myself, I can admit there have been expectations required of me and of them that were probably unreasonable at the time but necessary due to the needs of the business. The role of a front line manager as described by multiple companies I have worked for is *to provide a safe and organized environment, engage your team, manage the day to day operations by completing specified work orders, managing time and attendance, develop your associates, support teams, handle associate issues, escalate to HR and Sr. Leadership when necessary, reduce cost, stand for 10-12 hours, assist with physical work in the area as needed, stay flexible and adapt to changes in the operation timely, report hourly on the KPI's (key performance indicators), and oh yeah, have fun!* I have seen this firsthand how some managers are able to do this well and many others not so well. In fact, the managers that have done well either get promoted, burn out, or switch departments because of the expectations set upon them. I heard comments like, "these people are crazy." Has anyone ever said that?

As mentioned earlier, the role of a manger may take a different view depending on the organization. What I have found that best works for defining the role of the front-line manager for an organization is for the middle and senior leadership to **shadow** the front-line leaders in your company and understand what goes on daily. Many leaders will find that their front-line managers are faced with a mountain of challenges that they cannot easily overcome alone. They need your help and the best way to help them is to understand what they are doing, work to remove barriers in their way, streamline their work with them, and show them you care.

To summarize and meld the collective understanding of what a front-line manager's role is, below is what a front-line manager role encompasses:

> **Coach and Develop a Team**: A manager must be able to understand their business, create a plan, and develop a team that can accomplish any task. The primary goal is to coach and develop individuals from an "I" or "Me" mentality to a "We" and "Us." Managers must take their knowledge, skill, passion and strategically find a way to disseminate those attributes across various leaders in the organization.
>
> **Enable others**: As a leader in any organization, continuous improvement is needed to achieve upward mobility. A Front-Line Manager must empower their associates to explore without fear of failing; a list of lessons learned from failed attempts is still a win. They must know that their manager supports them and enables them to have a curious mind. The skill of enabling others is delicate and powerful. The leaders should provide support but don't remove the responsibility from the person.

Communication Skills: A Front-Line Manager must be capable to communicate. Communication to Sr. Leaders and associates is key in this level of leadership. They must be able to transpose information in a manner that is clear and concise and deliver specific levels of communication to the appropriate audience. You don't tell a two-year-old the meaning of life, you wait until they are 16 because they know everything.

Problem Solving: A Front-Line Manager should understand where an issue is coming from, how to triage it and what was the root cause. The Front-Line manager tends to be the first line of defense and must be able to identify the areas of risk quickly and eliminate it. This is supercritical when dealing with associates because they will come to the manger with problems of various types and sizes but it's the managers job to figure out how to solve them. The method used in solving the problem can and should vary but the responsibility ultimately lies with the manager.

Adapt to change: A Front-Line Manager should have an open mind and be flexible to changes in the operation and their environment. They should understand that yesterday's solutions don't always work for today's problems. Supervisors that are able to respond to change by having flexibility in their thinking, offering solutions, and leveraging their resources have a high likelihood of being successful in any organization. Not many people have home phones anymore, cell phones are predominantly used and soon, that will change also.

Why are Managers Needed

When you look at a team of any kind the makeup is very similar. Their are Players and Coaches. In Supply Chain, Managers have similar roles as Coaches in that they are responsible for not only winning - achieving the company goals. They are also responsible for the personal development of the associate they are entrusted with. Among all the lists and needs that are developed for why Managers are needed in any organization, I have seen the impact of having and not having Managers in place. Managers are needed to shepherd the flock. They are needed to cultivate the area of focus and promote growth and quality of life not just the results of winning. When Managers are in a position to lead their team and focus on fundamentals and build upon that, trust grows. Associates will begin to have a sense of loyalty to that manager and that is where discretionary effort takes over. Have you ever wondered how the same group of associates can deliver a better result with Manager A vs Manager B? When I look back at how Manager A has success with the same group of associates, I find more care for the associates from the Managers perspective and in turn more care for the Manager from the associates. This is something you cannot see physically but you can see this in action.

CHAPTER 3

Challenges and Successes
of Managers

Daily Operations

Challenges come in all shapes and sizes and most often when you don't want them. From my experience, managers have challenges dealing with the ambiguity of the day coupled with poor performance driven by a multitude of factors most of which may or may not be in their control. So, how does a manager or supervisor balance the pendulum of what my manager needs me to do, what the associates need, what they know needs to be done, and what can get done today. It's tough! Does it have to be? Certainly not!

The challenges of a Front-Line Manager are in their ability to identify areas of opportunities. Too many managers suffer in silence. They underutilize their capacity to truly conduct a self-evaluation and categorize leadership gaps. I have learned to think that this inability is a learned behavior rather than a gap in skill set. Typically, there is an Operations Manager or some mid-senior level leadership that is between the Front-Line Manager and the Director or General Manager. Often times, the level of leadership that is closest to the operation is told to 'just do' vs 'just think'. I have heard it said that managers shouldn't check their brains at the door when they get to work, but do we really ask or want their input? This is a question that if asked in your organization will shed light on your engagement scores. Leadership at the closest point to the operation is so important they are often times told what to do vs asked what should we do. Empowering this level of leadership will turn challenging managers into successful leaders.

Leaders experience many challenges. Over my 20 year career I have witnessed challenges such as time management, sustainability in projects, people interaction, focus and influencing peers and Sr. Leaders. It would baffle me how leaders would clam up around higher levels of leadership. As I was promoted to various levels in Supply Chain, I began to see how leaders treated me differently because my title and responsibility changed. Many discussions have been had with leaders about their inability to speak to Sr. Leaders and stay focused on processes or projects. I did get some advice from a retired Army Colonel that worked with me. He told me to stop saying but. If you are going to deliver a positive message don't come back with a but and say what you don't like. Leave the message where it is. As I valued that feedback and took to heart what was said, I realized just how much my messages were negative with positive spin offs. As a parent, I would not tell my child their "C" grade was good, but... you can do better. My approach would be totally different and this was a lesson well learned.

How to Manage my Manager

As I mentioned earlier, managers sometimes have challenges with focus. One of the best illustrations I could share is about a profession that requires 100% focus. Let's look at how a tightrope walker does their job. They make it look easy. When you speak to a tightrope walker, they will tell you they don't look down. They keep their eyes fixed on where they are going. Many tightrope walkers have said, if you look down your head will go that way and it's a good chance your body will also. So, their focus is to not look at the negative but to focus on where they are going. Throughout my career I have seen managers fail because they are focused on what isn't going right with their team, the leadership, and their ability to make change. Focus on what is going right. Focus on what is going well and the more you do that; your energy and effort will cause your actions to naturally gravitate towards the positive.

This also applies for Sr. Leaders. It may be difficult to digest that P&L may be -2 % to plan this month, but your turnover reduced by 48%. Your controllable costs have improved year over year by 12 basis points. Your site had zero OSHA recordables last month and now has momentum leading into the next month. How much more successful would the team be if we all spoke to our wins and focused our conversation on how to win more? I am not suggesting to neglect the opportunities or misses from any metric. How to manage up or manage your manager? It is all in the approach.

Leaders need to understand it is your responsibility to tell your story. There will always be an opportunity to do something better or differently. There will alway be a miss. If you can learn to tell your story than others won't have to tell your story for you. If you don't tell your story, someone will.

How to Win

Keeping inline with this thought, Managers must be focused on the goals of the company. The KPIs, internal process metrics, and milestones need to be visually seen so that the team can achieve them. If they keep this in their line of sight, their actions, thoughts, and conversations will gravitate towards those goals. Negative talk isn't accepted. Keep your focus on the goals and your team will follow the leader. A successful Front-Line manager will lead his/her team to victory. They will be the person that peers go to vs. their manager. They will act as an in-house consultant SME (Subject Matter Expert) when it comes to large or small projects. They will be able to influence others without playing a political game. Success for managers may look different depending on the company, industry, and individual. Some companies use monetary rewards to drive or foster success in managers. Often money is used as a strategy to improve "retention" within the management team. Other companies use comp. days, sports tickets, company paid dinners, and open recognition during manager meetings as a rewarding system to drive continual success with managers/supervisors.

There are many ways success is defined and understood for managers when KPI's are achieved, and daily deliverables are obtained. Most managers I have encountered would prefer the occasional accolades from their leader saying they appreciate their efforts. In my dealings with front line managers, some were very appreciative of these rewards while others said help me get my work day to 8 hours and that will be a huge win for me. Some describe success as incremental improvement day over day. Others describe success as the ability to bring value out of a challenging situation. I view a successful as someone that can have their team have an "Ah-ha" moment. Ah-ha as in they get it. The process makes sense and the team is starting to embrace the direction of the company. For this to happen, it requires meaningful conversation that the person or group understands, and they can now execute at a high level of accuracy and consistency.

CHAPTER 4

What makes a "good" Manager

Know your People

"A good manager is someone who inspires employees to perform optimally out of respect, not out of obligation. Good managers typically demonstrate a high degree of empathy and consideration for employees, but they balance these qualities with discipline and communication skills to meet deadlines." (1) That sounds good, but is this practical?

I believe it is practical and in this book, the concept I propose will allow managers to self-reflect on how they manage and what they can do to become good managers. Many of us would like to think we are good managers, but are we? Do we have a high degree of empathy and consideration for our employees? Do we balance these qualities with discipline and communication skills to meet deadlines? Are WE really teaching our associates and helping them become better people not just employees? Are we being shepherds of the flock. Take a moment and think about situations you have encountered that you could have and should have had more empathy, more consideration, or issued disciplinary action. Was the deadline met? Did you communicate well enough prior to missing the deadline, or was the project completed and not all the stakeholders were updated to the progress?

What do you define as a good manager? My understanding of a "good" manager is someone who possesses the ability to process an issue one inch wide and a mile deep on processes, problems, and solutions. In other words, someone that has a high sense of ownership, they can deliver results, they can develop their team, their team is inspired by the actions of the manager, and the manager has the trust of the organization. A test I use to measure how well the managers ability to execute as described is to require the manager to leave their department without a replacement. If the manager has given proper care and developed their associates, the team will continue to execute at a high level of accuracy. These managers are called "Best in Class" and can set clear expectations and their teams are able to execute at high levels.

For any manager to achieve this, they must be personally invested in their team, in the operation, and in the company. The manager must take time to work on developing informal leaders in their group. Building each individual up to a level to have the same confidence, empowerment and business aptitude they that is required to execute at a high level. When all this comes into play, the "good" manager is deemed trustworthy through their ability to manage a team regardless of the size, and they must be trusted to make the best decision based on Safety, Quality, People and Production.

I have seen several "good" managers in my career and most of them showed their greatness in challenging situations. At one company I worked for, there was a manager that was able to articulate to me daily what his hourly productivity was, where he was with completion of picking and loading, which associates were underperforming that day, and what is expected attrition looked like for the week relative to the forecasted volume. This guy was on the ball. He was super engaged with his team and had gained their respect. One thing he didn't do was go pick and load for them. He managed by walking around and talked to the associates in the work area. When he saw that his associates had barriers he actively and aggressively removed them. He also worked issues through his Coordinator keeping her abreast of the workflow as he saw it. They had a symbiotic relationship. See, he realized that part of his success what contingent upon how well he worked with and through his team. Taking this approach to leading his team I quickly saw turn over reduce, people that normally leave early diminish, HR issues subside, safety incidents go to zero, and productivity increase. The only thing I had to do was make sure his direct manager was removing barriers out of his way and supporting him where he needed.

Have a clear and well defined plan

Take five to seven minutes and list out your roadmap for how you plan. Think about the things you have learned throughout the year and have picked up from a person or two. Once you list out how you personally plan your day or your organization, think about how your leaders plan. Can you outline some of the thought processes and attributes of how your leaders plan? As a Front - Line Manager you should also understand how your team plans. In the absence of a Manager, informal leaders are always present. How do they plan and adjust to the flow of the day to drive the desired outcome? Having a well defined plan is a bigger deal than many people realize. A well defined plan man not be a detailed all inclusive plan but the plan allows the interpreter to make decisions that will help keep the business on track.

Here is a situation that happened and happens quite often. The Manager of a department of about 30 - 40 people had to take an associate to the on-site doctor or assist with addressing the medical issue with the associate. This situation requires the manager to leave their area of responsibility all the while still fully responsible for what is happening in their absence. Upon return, the manager realizes that they are 45-50 minutes behind on production. Several associates have taken additional bathroom breaks, and there is a mechanical issue that has been going on for 30 minutes and no one alerted maintenance. Having a well defined plan in this case would allow for informal leaders to make certain decisions to support the operation. The moment the manager leaves the area, maintenance could be notified so that a technician could patrol the area and be on standby. A supervisor or manager from another area could also split their time between their department and this one to give oversight and care to the associates. Targeted informal leaders can be engaged and deployed to help support the operation and are key in having a plan.

Know your business and have compassion

It should go without saying that knowing your business is a large portion of being a good manager. Here is another test you can do right now to see how well you know your business. Pretend you are in a classroom full of 2nd graders. Explain what you do so that they understand it. Can you speak to what is happening in the industry? Are you able to articulate the Companies direction for the next 3-5 years and explain your part in that vision? Can you tell those kids in that moment why it is important to learn problem solving skills at this critical age and how that translates into the workforce? Knowing your business is just that, know yous business.

I worked with a guy that was a Supervisor for a manufacturing company and he knew his business. The organizational structure of this company was very flat as there was the Owner and a few Supervisors. So inherently, everyone had a higher sense of ownership and understanding about the business. One day I witness something that helped me understand why knowing your business is so important and why so many people overlooked it. During the typical morning huddle around the whiteboard, I overheard a conversation that normally doesn't happen between a Supervisor and a Sr. Leader. I heard pushback. The Supervisor was defending why he was unable to process the produce the product in the manner requested. He was tactful but passionate. He explained the limitations of the equipment and even the physical specifications of the product and how it behaves. But he didn't stop there. He gave a solution which is probably why manager Sr. Leaders feel their managers do not know their business. As he gave his solution, it caused the Owner to think. I could only imagine what was going through his mind but what I saw was gratitude and frustration.

As I spoke with the Owner afterwards, I explained what I saw and thanked him for letting that play out in front of me. I asked him what the frustration was for vs. the gratitude. He told me the frustration was multifaceted. He said that his manager should have come with a solution well before that conversation happened. Also, why did it take having that conversation to get that result out of his leader. His gratitude was centered sole on the fact his leader had a solution and didn't need him to think for him. Knowing your business is super important and not just for the Leadership at the production or manufacturing ground level. The organization benefits when this level of leadership knows and understands so that pushback can happen and creative thought along with solutions can thrive.

CHAPTER 5

The Role of a Teacher

Setting the Tone

Teachers are our leaders in the classroom and many teachers serve multiple purposes. As I researched my kids teachers and multiple sources on the internet, I have found that some teachers set the tone for their classrooms. Other teachers make a point to build an environment where the students feel comfortable learning. Many teachers are mentors and provide a level of nurture to students where needed. It's almost a given that some teachers have become and are becoming precious role models in students' lives and as they engage with their students they build relationships. What does it mean to set the tone? When I think of this phrase, I am reminded of my childhood days playing baseball. The coach would tell the leadoff hitter, his job was to "set the tone". Our coach was a unique individual to say the least but like many Coaches he had nuggets of wisdom packed away in years and years of stuff. Setting the tone from his perspective was to let the other team know this is who we are. This is the pace in which we run our bases and field our plays. Setting the tone meant revealing our culture. Teachers likewise have to set the tone for their classrooms and the learning environment.

Think about how your leadership style and how your environment operates. What type of tone are you setting? What culture exists with you leading your team members or associates versus another leader. Is there a difference and if so why? Should there be a difference in the tone that is set within the same building? As we transition our thinking to managers as teachers, setting the tone and establishing the culture wanted verses the culture present is largely dependent on the engagement of the manager. Inspect what you expect.

Planning

Needless to say, teachers have a tall task in front of them and most take it with stride. Teachers are given a set of students from varying backgrounds, ethnic groups, and learning capabilities that they must figure out how to motivate, educate, and inspire to become more than they were from the first day of school. This is a very complex process with state and federal regulated guidelines that must be followed. Teachers are given a curriculum that they must follow to meet state requirements. From this curriculum, lesson plans are created and keep in mind, these lesson plans are not tailor made to each student. Teachers create tests and pop quizzes, classroom expectations and standards, track student performance, have regularly scheduled meetings with parents for progress updates and further support, manage students outside of normal classroom activity such as lunch period, recess, in school suspension, and general student behavior as they are entrusted to the school system daily. Teachers are also counselors and because some have a close relationship with their students they can uncover problems and issues that parents may not notice and bring out the greatness in our children.

Creating a healthy environment

The role of a teacher is so important, it is the very fabric of our society and often overlooked as a critical role in the development of the next generation. Some students mimic and imitate their teacher's behavior and actions so by understanding this, we get a grasp of how ingrained teachers are with students that will eventually become tomorrow's workforce. When a teacher can create an inviting, safe, happy environment, the students are more apt to learn and be an active participant within the classroom. The environment, this controlled work area is established and maintained by the teacher. Many of us have head the minicom, happy wife happy life, the same would be true for a teacher. If the teacher is happy, engaging, prepared, and ready to handle 20-30 different personalities every day, the learning environment becomes less impaired and more conducive of productive learning. The inverse is also true. When teachers are not engaging, distraught because they can't buy the things needed to make the classroom more inviting, and they aren't prepared to deliver a lesson plan due to a lack of materials or possible parental support, the learning environment will be challenging and students that may excel are put at further disadvantages.

I have had the privilege of teachers mentoring me because they saw something worth developing. This mentorship wasn't asked for on my part but was given through the subtle ways teachers coax students into doing more with less, being creative, and praising students even in the smallest of achievements. Encouraging students in the classroom setting to enjoy learning and feeling ok to show vulnerability is key to building confidence and social skills that often go overlooked in today's working environment. Later, we will explore how managers and supervisors possess the same power and control in their working environment and can bring greatness out of their associates through engagement, well defined planning and execution, meaningful conversation, and a willingness to listen and grow with their team. By understanding this comparison, hopefully this will allow front-line managers the mental framework they need to build their confidence and help them want to be successful.

What makes a "good" Teacher

Compassion

Many of us have had "good" teachers. Remember the definition of "good"? (3). Good is defined as someone of a favorable character, morally right, kind, benevolent, deserving of respect, honorable. Teachers have inspired many of us to do more and become more than we ever thought. Good teachers can build relationships with us that have transcended past school age. Bonds were formed, and loyalty was built. Some of the teachers that are deemed as good have the innate ability to see through us metaphorically and speak in our language and meet us at our level. They are counselors. They are gap fillers. They are compassionate. This compassion is often felt and not seen. Many teachers will tell you they do more for their students that go unnoticed and unsaid than people realize. They do this because they care. At the core of the day, the teacher that is compassionate cares more about the student learning and being better than getting noticed or rewarded. Question to ask yourself, are you compassionate about the team you lead?

Trust & Integrity

We could spend an entire session on trust and integrity with teachers and leaders. As a parent I cannot put a value on trust and integrity with teachers that influence my childrens' lives. Thinking through this should help provide more framework around what a good leader means to you. A "good" teacher can be defined as one that has empathy, open-mindedness, integrity, organized, engaging, enthusiastic, a good communicator, subject matter expert, and knows your name. Think about a teacher you had that was a "good" teacher. List the qualities they had that qualified them as good and understand how they used them. What was so significant about this teacher that made an impact on your life? Are you better now because of your involvement with this teacher? As you think about the characteristics and attributes of a good teacher make a list of what sticks out to you. Now, ask yourself how you compare to the attributes you listed. Many of us will realize that we have some bad habits that need immediate correction, and there are some attributes or characteristics that we need to embody from the good teachers we have had the pleasure of learning from.

Inspiration

Good teachers like good managers are not born, they are created. Through extensive training, development, and experiences, untapped potential is pulled out of these individuals and they begin to excel in their profession. The thing to understand is this doesn't happen overnight. It takes persistence and determination to hone in on the craft of engaging people, developing plans, empowering your team, and leveraging diversity within our organization to drive the desired outcome. What is inspiration and why is this important? Inspiration is defined many ways by various intellectual institutions. I define inspiration as the ability or process of being either physically or mentally motivated to do or feel something. I had a teacher that inspired me when I was in seventh grade. Mr. Hair. He had a way about calling on me to come to the chalkboard to write out the algebra answers. He was our pre-algebra teacher and he knew that the kids in the class were terrified of learning math at this level at such a young age. His methodology was to write a problem on the board and talk through the solution. Once he was done, he called upon a random student to write out the solution. Many times I was called and rose to that challenge but I did not understand all the behind the scenes things that were happening to me. I assumed I was just answering a problem on a chalkboard. Mr. Hair inspired me to do more and not be afraid to stand in front of my peers. He removed nervousness. Uncovered timidity. He build trust with me.

CHAPTER 7

The Concept!

What is it!

Managers are teachers. In some capacity every manager must teach their team and the better their ability to teach their team exists, the expectation is that the team should perform at standard. I suggest, training managers like teachers so that the skill of teaching is engrained in managers and the environment can have a positive shift where improvement in employee relations, turnover reduction for associates and management, and improvement in work life balance using better planning and execution. Training managers like teachers should not be a surprise to anyone but should be a reality for everyone.

Many companies have experienced growing pains and have reached out to manager training organizations to get their managers trained on basic leadership. So, this is known industry wide that there is a gap in training, leadership skills, or even the ability to get front-line managers the skill and thinking ability to execute how the company wants. Many people call this leadership 101. This guide is 1ˢᵗ hand information from the front line. I was there. My colleagues were there. I have worked side-by-side with almost 100 managers during my career and there is a theme that is consistent. As I managed people that needed a tool such as this, we experienced multiple issues from excessive attrition and turnover, work life balance, balancing with the company needs vs what the associates can do, you name it. There are no easy answers to these situations and the challenge can be daunting, but there are practical solutions that can be put in place to reduce turnover, improve employee relations, work life balance, and achieve daily deliverables.

If managers and supervisors lose the associates, you lose the building. Processes breakdown, labor budgets sky rocket, productivity and efficiency gains are diminished, and countless hours of process improvements or continuous improvement (CI) are put in place to fix what could have been avoided if the leadership was able to recognize problems and execute. It is critical for organizations to invest in and protect the front-line management. Being a football fan, I relate front - line management to Coordinators on a football team staff. It would be very hard for the Head Coach to deliver excellence and ultimately win the Super Bowl if investment wasn't made in the Coordinators. One of the most critical roles in Supply Chain is front-line managers and supervisors; Coordinators.

Why

The concept I propose is right in front of all of faces but hasn't been tapped into. It's managers thinking like teachers to deliver a better product. Think about this. Have you ever had a favorite teacher, or a teacher that had the biggest impact on your life? What qualities did they have? Were they extremely smart? Where they hypersensitive about goals? Or were they engaging? Did they call you out when you were lying and trying to bluff them? Did they bring greatness out of you! The latter is true for me. Mr. Hair, my seventh grade teacher put me on the spot multiple days and told me he believed in me and that made me not want to let him down. It made me happy to see my teacher smile with approval when I completed my goals. What caused that feeling? Why was there a sense of loyalty to this teacher above all others? As I rationalize this, I felt an obligation to do well because my teacher invested time and confidence in me and I knew that he wouldn't let me fail. I felt that I had a safety net of sorts with Mr. Hair that if I went to the chalkboard and began to struggle, he was right there to guide me and keep me from embarrassment. That caused me to step up and deliver when called upon.

I propose, he inspired me to be better. It is my belief that if managers would take an approach of a teacher they can have untapped gains in Supply Chain that transcend technological advancement and bring forth from their associates unprecedented gains in operational efficiency, productivity, reduce turnover, and company specific KPI's that have varying levels of inconsistency. It has been proven that when connections are made at the emotional level, breakthroughs happen that cannot be explained by conventional methods. The ability to make an emotional connection is often misunderstood because it's not about being emotional or showing emotion. When we make a human connection, it means something and that is a bond from one person to another.

There are a few steps that a manager should do to approach operations with a teacher like feel verses common practices. This concept is broken down into four fundamental elements.

First, understand the Key Performance Indicators: KPI's. Managers often struggle with understanding why certain things are measured or how they are measured. This is critical for the manager to understand the why because they have the most impact to influencing change to the deliverable or metric. If they understand it, they can work with their team through the planning process to drive the desired result. I have seen where the message of why gets lost in translation from Sr. Leaders to the Leadership in the work area. Validating the Manger understands why the metric is important and how the metric is calculated and what inputs are present that influences the KPI is groundbreaking important.

Secondly, create a detailed plan. Read the next appendix to understand how to create a detailed plan. The manager and supervisors should understand key factors that impact their business and make plans around them. Managers should plan for the known and the unexpected. Known factors that impact day to day businesses should be well defined and understood. This can be accomplished in planning meetings around a specific issue or topic. Things like expected volume versus actual volume. Roster headcount versus expected show attendance. Operational commodities like pallets, stretch film and other supplies that are used to process parts. Planning for what is known allows the team to think through possible issues days before it happens and allows them to adjust. They begin to visualize success and should be able to see what behaviors are necessary to achieve the goals.

Planning for the unexpected is called contingency planning. This is just as critical as planning for known issues. A technique I use is I list all the possible issues that could happen, assign a value to them so I can rank them, and then create countermeasures around each possible issue. This is technique is called Failure modes and effects analysis (FMEA), which is a step-by-step approach for identifying all possible failures in a design, a process, or a product or service.

Thirdly, set the environment. Just like in a classroom, the manager and the supervisor are the teacher. A critical part of their role is to create an environment that is safe, visual (people can see the expectations – write them down and post it), inviting (it doesn't look like it's lacking information), the relevant information is present, and the associate feels comfortable voicing concerns. Just like in a classroom, people should know where to go, when to go, how to get there, and when to leave. It should be clear to them what is expected, why it's expected, and how it impacts them. Managers and Teachers can deal with the ambiguity of the operation, associates and students should have clear rules of engagement.

Lastly, engage your team. Managers that can gain the respect, trust, and discretionary effort of the team have an engaged workforce. Managers should **meet people where they are**. In the arena of coaching, engaging, and developing their team or an individual, understanding where someone is on their development journey is critical. Meeting someone where they are simply means talking to them and understanding where they are mentally with their development or operation. When managers do this as teachers do every day, they are able to lay hold of the intangible unseen attributes of a person and develop them and drive the operation. This level of engagement fosters the associates desire to see their manager succeed. This is partly because the manager is constantly investing all the necessary tools, support, training, inspiration, and rewards to their department and associates. This process is so impactful, it will literally change the focus of how mid-level and sr. leaders interact with front-line managers.

DO IT!

Steps to train your Manager like a Teacher

If you are a manager or supervisor having challenges and want to improve your performance the first thing you need to do is calm down and understand you're not alone. Up to this point, you have been doing the best you can with the tools and understanding you have right now. As you have read in the prior chapters, we are going to take a different approach. Many supervisors and front-line managers are either overwhelmed by the scope of work or their ambitions and they are creating an unproductive environment for both themselves and the associates.

Teacher attributes like Manager attributes

1. Understand the KPIs and how to achieve them – Strategic Planning
   a. Curriculum = KPI's

There are many KPI's that companies utilized to drive performance. One of which is throughput, which is a measure of how efficient the operation is relative to labor hours and units processed. Here is an example: Today's volume is 13,000 units and we need to perform at a 125 UPH (units per hour).

Here is the equation:
Volume / Performance goal (UPH) = Total hours to use
13,000 / 125 UPH = 104 hours

Understanding the KPI for that specific area will allow the manager to make a better plan. I have experienced conversations with managers that led me to understand that they did not know how to plan or breakdown the KPI in simple form. This was a teaching moment which is the spirit of the book. Some Supervisors and managers have shortcomings by not having a plan well defined. From my experience, I have heard managers say they don't have time to plan. What would we do as parents if we heard from the teachers of our children say they didn't plan or have time to plan? How soon would we contact the principal and the school board complaining about this teacher. So why do we "accept" inability to plan at a strategic level. As managers gain an in-depth understanding of the company's goals and inputs drive the KPI's, the manager is now more able to make detailed planning at the department level.

2.   Plan - Lesson plan = Detailed Planning

Teachers try hard to have a well-defined and engaging lesson plans. What are most managers doing to make the mundane work fresh and exciting? As leaders supporting the managers, what are you doing to help the managers drive operational excellence? A manager should have corresponding lesson plan for their area that guides them to the pathway of success driven by the overarching KPI's. I have had the pleasure of working with some smart and detailed managers. One manager told me he doesn't focus on the KPI's, he focuses on the process metrics. As I dug into the meaning of process metrics, he stated that his team focuses on the fundamentals of blocking and tackling hour by hour and hitting those goals with the understanding that if they do the small things right, the big things will take care of themselves. Since this manager has shifted to this focus, his team is more organized, laser focused on what needs to be done hour by hour and has a high degree of accuracy and compliance with process accuracy and planning.

An example of detailed planning would be baking a cake. If you told your associates or your managers to write the steps to baking a cake, what would you get? I would assume you would get a myriad of variations and they all would start differently. Baking a cake is one of the simplest things you can do and the process is well defined. Assuming you have a place to bake the cake and the equipment to do so as well, the first thing I would do is get a cake box and look on the back. The directions are there and the process is there also. For some reason those smart people made some visuals so that people would be able to interpret the directions if they ran into any problems. How well does your team bake a cake?

Elements of an effective plan:

1. *Define the Mission/Purpose (what are you trying to accomplish)*
2. *State the problem (clear and concise)*
3. *Corrective action steps*
   a. *GEMBA the process first*
   b. *Use PDCA cycles to prove your hypothesis*
   c. *Document your activity*
4. *Measure/Track (determine how you will gauge success of the outputs and performance)*
5. *List stakeholders and team members*
   a. *Who's responsible – team lead*
   b. *Who's supporting the project – team resources*
6. *Tools & Support needed*
   a. *Define and list what tools are needed*
   b. *Define and list what support is needed outside of your job scope*
7. *Establish who will report out and the frequency*

3. Set the environment - Make the process visual
   a. Class room = Start-up Area
      It all starts at the Start up

People want to know what they are doing and how they measure up. Assuming positive intent, nobody comes to work to fail. People don't just wake up and say, I am going to really screw things up today. By making the process visual you create an environment for people to understand what they are to do, when they are to do it, and how it's supposed to be done.

Example, a teacher's classroom. Look at a pre-k to 3rd grade class room and then look at your start up area. Notice a difference? The classroom is 5S'd (Sort, Set, Shine, Standardize, Sustain), visually with what subject matter will be learned, even some disciplinary action is visible to the kids in the room. Take a hard look at your start up area and ask yourself, are you creating an environment for your associates to get the proper information? This is their "home room" per say so the startup area should be full of information and tools that the associates need with a focus on company goals.

4. Engage your team: Coaching is empowerment
    -   There is value in face to face interaction
    -   PTA = Round table meetings are (1:1's)
    -   DO NOT SUFFER IN SILENCE

Anyone in a leadership position must know who's on your team and must know where to best place people on your team. To *know* who's on your team is to have a meaningful relationship with them on a professional level. This can be a daunting task depending on the size of your team and the complexity of the operation, but this is probably the most critical aspect of this plan. Most people want to feel a sense of belonging. Associates and managers spend 40 plus hours per week at work and by having an engaged team, the manager or supervisor can achieve the plans and goals set by the organization. By engaging your team, you will understand how powerful, critical, and impactful, the gains in operation are outside of technological advancement and operational improvements which are derived by the untapped and often untouched discretionary effort.

In recent statistics, it has been estimated that $366 billion dollars was spent in 2018 in the arena of training. Can you imagine the billions of dollars are spent in the arena of manager development to teach managers how to engage their team and the importance of having an engaged team. This concept that is proposed to everyone is complex but simple and will save organizations millions of dollars. Think like a teacher, act like a manager. This will bridge the gap of the leadership to the associates that are entering and in the workforce. Embody the attributes and characteristics of a teacher and a manager will see personal growth and development with their team.

Note: The better prepared the teacher is builds credibility with the student and parent. Likewise, a prepared and organized manager builds trust and credibility with his or her associates and management team. As managers and supervisors are engaging their team credibility is key. You must demonstrate that you care, you have a well-defined plan, you are personable and approachable, and you can get feedback to the associates.

APPENDIX 2

Core factors Teachers learn, and Managers will gain

Teacher	Manager
Lesson plan	Strategic planning
Curriculum (kpi)	Site level KPI's
Classroom setting	Startup area
CE classes	Leader development
Teacher work days	Manager planning days
Relationships	Team building exercises
Work life balance	Work life balance

FAILURE MODE EFFECT ANALYSIS

When to Use FMEA

- When a process, product or service is being designed or redesigned, after quality function deployment.
- When an existing process, product or service is being applied in a new way.
- Before developing control plans for a new or modified process.
- When improvement goals are planned for an existing process, product or service.
- When analyzing failures of an existing process, product or service.
- Periodically throughout the life of the process, product or service

FMEA Procedure

(Again, this is a general procedure. Specific details may vary with standards of your organization or industry.)

1. Assemble a cross-functional team of people with diverse knowledge about the process, product or service and customer needs. Functions often included are: design, manufacturing, quality, testing, reliability, maintenance, purchasing (and suppliers), sales, marketing (and customers) and customer service.

2. Identify the scope of the FMEA. Is it for concept, system, design, process or service? What are the boundaries? How detailed should we be? Use flowcharts to identify the scope and to make sure every team member understands it in detail. (From here on, we'll use the word "scope" to mean the system, design, process or service that is the subject of your FMEA.)

3. Fill in the identifying information at the top of your FMEA form. Figure 1 shows a typical format. The remaining steps ask for information that will go into the columns of the form.

Function	Potential Failure Mode	Potential Effects(s) of Failure	S	Potential Cause(s) of Failure	O	Current Process Controls	D	R P N	C R I T	Recommended Action(s)	Responsibility and Target Completion Date	Action Taken	S	O	D	R P N	C R I T
Dispense amount of cash requested by customer	Does not dispense cash	Customer very dissatisfied Incorrect entry to demand deposit system Discrepancy in cash balancing	8	Out of cash	5	Internal low-cash alert	5	200	40								
				Machine jams	3	Internal jam alert	10	240	24								
				Power failure during transaction	2	None	10	160	16								
	Dispenses too much cash	Bank loses money Discrepancy in cash balancing	6	Bills stuck together	2	Loading procedure (riffle ends of stack)	7	84	12								
				Denominations in wrong trays	3	Two-person visual verification	4	72	18								
	Takes too long to dispense cash	Customer somewhat annoyed	3	Heavy computer network traffic	7	None	10	210	21								
				Power interruption during transaction	2	None	10	60	6								

REFERENCES

1. https://www.reference.com/business-finance/
   define-good-manager-b5fbb1bf5540a757
2. http://www.businessdictionary.com/definition/
   front-line-management.html
3. https://www.merriam-webster.com/dictionary/
   good
4. http://centerforcoachingexcellence.com/blog/
   emotional-connections
5. http://asq.org/learn-about-quality/process-analysis-
   tools/overview/fmea.html

ABOUT THE AUTHOR

David has over 20 years of Supply Chain and Manufacturing experience as various levels. He has lead teams through facility startups, warehouse management system changes, and workstream redesigns. He brings first hand ground floor experience as he has personally seen operations within multiple companies and has supervised managers from front-line positions to senior levels.

www.ingramcontent.com/pod-product-compliance
Lightning Source LLC
Chambersburg PA
CBHW051413250726
48655CB00003B/1016